Mini Instant Pot Cookbook

Quick, Healthy and Delicious Instant Pot Mini Recipes for 3 Quart Models

Jamie Stratton

Table of contents

Introduction

If you are a rising home chef, then you have definitely heard of a number of amazing cooking appliances such as the Air Fryer, Sous Vide circulators, Slow Cooker and of course, the amazing Instant Pot!

While all the other devices do have their own merits, the Instant Pot line of products stands on a level of its own!

They can easily be considered to be the epitome of Electric Pressure Cookers that boasts unsurpassed quality and versatility in terms of cooking.

However, just in case you don't know! The Instant Pot is an extremely robust and versatile Electric Pressure cooker that utilizes the power pressure cooking to prepare and cook meals almost 70% faster that other traditional cooking methods!

Not only that, the amazing array of pre-programmed modes and settings makes using the Instant Pot a total breeze!

Even if you are a complete novice in the field cooking, you will still be able to create magnificent dishes with the help your pot!

You should know now that there are actually multiple variations of the Instant Pot. However, the recipes found in this book are perfect for the Instant Pot Mini Duo, which is the smallest (and possibility cutest) version of the Instant Pot that comes with extreme portability without sacrificing any of the power!

To make things as accessible as possible, I have divided this book into multiple chapters that are further broken into small bite sections for you to absorb.

The first few chapters of the book focuses on giving you a brief overview of the Instant Pot basics while the rest focus on the amazing 50+ healthy recipes found in this book!

I sincerely hope that you will find the contents of this book beneficial and helpful in the long run!

Chapter 1: Instant Pot Mini Basics

When the Instant Pot was first designed by the Canadians, the core objective was to make sure that the device is as much "Convenient" and "Accessible" as possible.

It was designed to speed up cooking by almost 6 times and save a lot of energy in the process while perfectly preserving the nutrients of the meal.

Throughout the years there have been several iterations of the Instant Pot since its conception! But when looking at the Pot from the perspective of convenience, perhaps no other model beats the portability and ease of use of the Instant Pot Duo Mini!

This particular 3-quart model is perfect for individuals who are always on the go!

Whether you are a student who needs to prepare quick meals, or a member of a small family! The Instant Pot Duo Mini perfectly fits the bill when trying preparing simple side dishes, rice meals, vegetables and even main dishes in small quantities!

The small form factor is accompanied with the fact that it emits very little amount of steam/ cooking smell or heat, which also makes it a perfect travelling companion! Staying at a hotel and want to cook meals in your room? No problem!

The fully enclosed environment of the Pot helps to trap the nutrient, aroma and flavors of the meal instead of releasing them all around! This allows the pot to create meals that are extremely healthy and rich in flavor.

And the best part? If you do things right, you will always get consistent results with the pot!

What exactly is an Instant Pot?

Before explaining what, an Instant Pot is, we must first understand what "Pressure Cooking" actually means.

Moving all of the technical jargon aside, pressure cooking is essentially a process of cooking meals in a sealed-up vessel by trapping/generating steam inside of it.

Modern day pressure cookers such as the Instant Pot are designed in such an elegant and technologically way that even the minutest amount of steam generation can be controlled using different parameters.

As to "How" pressure cookers work, they actually follow a very simple law of physics.

Simply put the boiling point of water increases as the pressure increases.

When it comes an Instant Pot, as more and more steam is being generated inside, the pressure eventually increases. This leads to the water reaching very high temperatures without actually boiling up or evaporating which helps the device to greatly minimize the time taken to prepare the meals.

Basic Features of Instant Pot Duo Mini

The basics features of the Instant Pot Duo Mini are as follows:

7 In 1 Multi Cooker: The Mini Duo is an excellent and versatile device that has the power to act as a Pressure Cooker, Rice Cooker, Porridge Cooker, Slow Cooker, Yogurt Maker, Steamer, Warmer and even a Sauté Pan!

Extremely User-Friendly LED Screen: The user-friendly LED display shows all the information that you need during the cooking period.

11 Smart Built-In-Programs: There are multiple built-in programs that make the cooking experience more enjoyable and seamless. These are explained in details in Chapter 2.

Simple and Accessible Program Adjustments: The accessible nature of the buttons helps to adjust the settings seamlessly, even while cooking!

Dual Pressure Settings: The Dual Pressure setting allows for fast and flexible cooking experience. The High-pressure mode reduces cook time by 70% while the Low-pressure mode helps to cook delicate foods.

Stainless Steel Cooking Pot: The Stainless-Steel Cooking Pot is food grade 304 (18/8) that contains no chemical coatings. It has markings at ½ and 2/3 lines to act as a guide when filling the pot. The inner pot is dishwasher safe as well!

High Quality Exterior: The exterior of the device is made of Brushed Stainless Steel that is finger print resistant! It comes with a lid holder that allows both left and right-handed users to use the device.

The structure of the pot explained

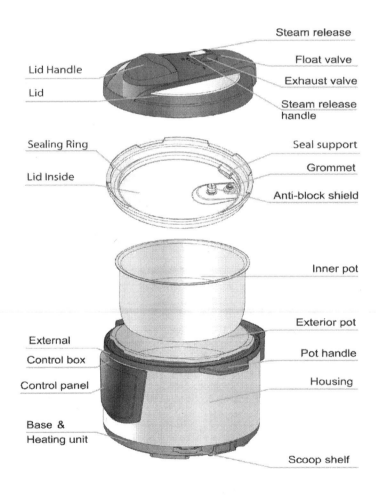

Different manufacturers of electric pressure cookers tend to add/remove something from the device to make it "unique".

However, there are some features that are staple to almost every electric pressure cooker out there.

The most basic Electric Pressure Cooker unit consists of

- a pressure cooker pot which is also known as the inner pot/cooking pot
- the electric heating elements which provides the actual heat
- Electronically controlled temperature and pressure sensors

The heating process of the cooker is carefully regulated by the temperature and pressure sensors that are installed in the housing itself.

Speaking in scientific terms though, electric pressure cookers tend to cook by following a process known as "Closed Loop Control System"

Modern electric pressure cookers usually contain a number of different "Pre-Determined" settings which are initialized after going through intensive research regimes. The pre-determined programs help to easily set the most optimal settings for warming, cooking rice, braising etc. to bring about the best possible result.

For all of these different features, Instant Pots are said to be "Multi Talented Programmable Cooking Device"

Chapter 2: The Instant Pot Mini Button

The Instant Pot is an amazing and versatile device! But the myriad of buttons present in the pot might be rather confusing to some.

To avoid something similar happening to you, here's a list of the main buttons of the Pot and a brief summary of their functions.

- Sauté: You should go for this button if you want to simply sauté your vegetables or produces inside your inner pot while keeping the lid opened. It is possible to adjust the level of brownness you desire by pressing the adjust button as well. As a small tip here, you can very easily press the Sauté Button followed by the Adjust Button two times to simmer your food.

- Keep Warm/Cancel: Using this button, you will be able to turn your pressure cooker off. Alternatively, you can use the adjust button to keep maintaining a warm temperature ranging from 145-degree Celsius (at normal) to 167 (at more) degree Celsius depending on what you need.

- Manual: This is pretty much an all-rounder button which gives a greater level of flexibility to the user. Using this button followed by the + or – buttons, you will be able to set the exact duration of cooking time which you require.

- Soup: This mode will set the cooker to a high-pressure mode giving 30 minutes of cooking time (at normal); 40 minutes (at more); 20 minutes (at less)

- Meat/Stew: This mode will set the cooker to a high-pressure mode giving 35 minutes of cooking time (at normal); 45 minutes (at more); 20 minutes (at less)

- Bean/Chili: This mode will set the cooker to a high-pressure mode giving 30 minutes of cooking time (at normal); 40 minutes (at more); 25 minutes (at less)

- Rice: This is a fully automated mode which cooks rice on low pressure. It will adjust the timer all by itself depending on the amount of water/rice present inside the inner cooking pot.

- Porridge: This mode will set the cooker to a high-pressure mode giving 20 minutes of cooking time (at normal); 30 minutes (at more); 15 minutes (at less)

- Steam: This will set your pressure cooker to high pressure with 10 minutes cooking time at normal. 15 minutes cook time at more and 3 minutes cook time at less. Keep in mind that it is advised to use this mode with a steamer basket or rack for best results.

- Slow Cooker: This button will normally set the cooker at 4-hour mode. However, you change the temperature by keeping it at 190-201-degree Fahrenheit (at low); 194-205-degree Fahrenheit (at normal); 199-210-degree Fahrenheit (at high);

- Pressure: This button allows you to alter between high and low-pressure settings.

- Yogurt: This setting should be used when you are in the mood for making yogurt in individual pots or jars

- Timer: This button will allow you to either decrease or increase the time by using the timer button and pressing the + or – buttons

Chapter 3: Amazing Advantages of Instant Pot and Basic Instructions

You must be pretty stoked right about now to explore the recipes, right? Just a little longer now!

Let me give you a breakdown of the advantages you will enjoy while using your Instant Pot Mini.

- Let's first start with the time! I have already mentioned this before, but the utilizing the power of pressure cooking actually allows you to increase your cooking time by almost 70%! This frees up a lot of time in your daily routine.
- The process of pressure cooking requires much less liquid, which helps to perfectly preserve the nutritional values of the meals, making meals extremely healthy!
- Electric Pressure Cookers such as the Instant Pot are extremely intelligent and are able to seamlessly control and regulate the internal temperature automatically and create the best suitable environment for your meals. These automated functionalities make Electric Pressure cookers extremely versatile and easy to use. Not to mention, extremely safe!
- The Instant Pot will allow you to prepare "One Pot" meals! This basically means that the Instant Pot allows you to prepare meals by simply adding the ingredients to the pot. The pot takes care of the remaining process. This allows you to quickly cook meals such as pasta, chili or stews! And since everything is made in a single pot, cleaning won't be a hassle either!
- Since the pot takes much less time to cook your meals, you will be able to save a good amount of electricity and save a lot of money on that front.

Basic Guidelines of Using the Pot

Despite the popularity, there are some misconceptions that using an Instant Pot might be extremely difficult!

The truth is the exact opposite though!

The following steps will briefly illustrate the core working procedure of the Instant Pot. It might vary a little depending on the recipe, but the main procedure remains the same.

- If your recipe calls ingredients such as vegetables, condiments or meats to be Sautéed, you can simply use the SAUTE mode and add the ingredients and Sate them in a bit of oil as needed.
- Once the Sautéing is done, add the remaining ingredients and close lid
- Turn the STEAM handle to sealing position
- Select your pressure level according to the recipe and set timer
- The pot will take care of the rest!
- Once the pressure cooking cycle is complete, the display will show "KEEP WARM". At this point, you have to release the pressure.
- Now, there are two ways you can release the pressure, either a quick release or a natural release. Both of them have their perks that are discussed below.
- Once the pressure is released, open the lid and simmer the meal (In Sauté mode) if needed and serve!

Easy right?

Now, let me talk a little bit about the Pressure Release Mechanism of the pot.

The first one is the Quick Release pressure and the second is Natural Pressure Release.

Let's a talk a bit about Quick Release first.

Quick Pressure Release: Once the cook timer reaches zero, you have the option to release all the pressure at once! This will stop further cooking and prevent overcooking.

This is suitable for sensitive ingredients such as seafood or vegetables. However, keep in mind that quick release is a bit risky as a lot of steam comes out at once, so be sure to stay alert when releasing steam via this method.

Natural Pressure Release: The Natural Pressure Release will require you to wait to 10-30 minutes after the cooking is complete and allow the Instant Pot to release the pressure itself. Once "KEEP WARM" lights up in the display, it basically means that your pot is now release the pressure.

If you want then you can wait for the whole 30 minutes, or you can simply wait for 10 minutes and perform a Quick Release.

Foods that are high in liquid volume or are starchy calls for a Natural Pressure Release. Alternatively, large cuts of meat may also require you to release pressure naturally as to ensure proper and even cooking.

Chapter 4: Common Mistakes to Avoid

Below are some time tables that are designed to give you a rough idea of the cooking time required for various ingredients and food items. However, before you dive into the recipes, there are a few things that you should know-

For Meat: When considering to use RAW meat, you should always make sure to never leave them at room temperature for 2 hours. Also, when using delayed cooking, make sure to not set the timer for than 1-2 hours.

For Veggies: When steaming your vegetables, use at least 2 cups of water and a free-standing vegetable steamer or wire mesh basket set on the provided trivet. Make sure to Quick release the pressure to avoid overcooking.

For Fruits: When steaming your fruits, use at least 2 cups of water and a free-standing vegetable steamer or wire mesh basket set on the provided trivet. Make sure to Quick release the pressure to avoid overcooking.

How to make other recipes Instant Pot friendly

The versatile nature of the Instant Pot allows you to prepare a multitude of different types of recipes!

However, you might still be interested to convert some of the normal recipes and make them Instant Pot compatible. If that's the case, the following pointers will help you-

- Since the pressure cooker doesn't allow for evaporation like stove top cookers, it is wise to minimize the amount of liquid used. Just used as much as barely needed, however don't go below 1 cup!
- You have to keep in mind that the time taken for cooking the meal will significantly get reduced. A general rule of thumb is to cut down your cooking time by $2/3^{rd}$ of the original recipe. However, a better way to calculate this is the compare the ingredients that you are using with the cooking time table provided above.

- The general rule for adding dairy when it comes to an Instant Pot is at the end of the cooking session. This is to avoid excess foaming and scorching, which might hamper the flavor of your dish.
- If you plan on adding something like a cornstarch mixture to thicken your sauce, then it is advised that you add after the cooking is complete. Set your pot to Sauté mode and add your thickener if needed

Early Mistakes to Avoid

By now most of the basics of Instant Pot are pretty much covered! Before letting you go wild on the recipes, let me give you a final few pointers that will help you to avoid early mistakes.

- If you are planning to deglaze your pot, use the Sauté button
- Try to experiment as much as possible during your free time. It will help you understand the work flow of Instant Pot better and help you create amazing meals.
- If you are facing a bit confusion, make sure to either consult this brief handbook or the official Instant Pot handbook before trying to fix things by yourself.
- When you are dealing with large amounts of food, always make sure to avoid using the QUICK RELEASE button as it might cause the pot to spray hot liquid
- When release Stove Top pressure cookers, some people often tend to run it under cold water and release the pressure. However, since we are working with electricity here, that is a very harmful practice and you should avoid doing that at all cost
- If you ever happen to double the size of your recipe, make sure to NOT double the time as well! since the Instant Pot tends to cook all food at the same rate. More of the same food does not mean more time required.

Chapter 5: Breakfast Recipes

Yummy Quiche

Serving: 2

Prep Time: 10 minutes

Cook Time: 30 minutes

Ingredients

- 1 cup water
- 3 whole eggs
- ¼ cup milk
- Pinch of salt and pepper
- 1 tablespoon of chives, chopped
- ½ a cup of cheddar cheese, shredded
- Cooking spray as needed

How To

1. Take a bowl and add egg, salt, pepper, chives and milk
2. Whisk well
3. Wrap a cake pan with tin foil
4. Grease with cooking spray and add cheese
5. Pour egg mix over cheese and spread
6. Add water to your Instant Pot
7. Add steamer basket inside
8. Add cake pan and close lid
9. Cook on HIGH pressure for 30 minutes
10. Release the pressure naturally over 10 minutes
11. Divide between 2 plates and enjoy!

Nutrition (Per Serving)

- Calories: 214
- Fat: 4g
- Carbohydrates: 7g
- Protein: 8g

Bacon and Potatoes

Serving: 2

Prep Time: 10 minutes

Cook Time: 7 minutes

Ingredients

- ½ a pound red potato, cubed
- 1 bacon strip, chopped
- 1 teaspoon parsley, dried
- A pinch of salt and pepper
- ½ a teaspoon garlic powder
- 1 and ½ ounce cheddar cheese, grated
- 1-ounce ranch dressing
- 1 tablespoon water

How To

1. Add potatoes, bacon, parsley, salt, garlic powder, pepper, water to your Instant Pot and stir
2. Close lid and cook on HIGH pressure for 7 minutes
3. Release the pressure naturally over 10 minutes
4. Open lid and stir in cheese and dressing
5. Toss and divide the mix between 2 plates
6. Serve and enjoy!

Nutrition (Per Serving)

- Calories: 258
- Fat: 2g
- Carbohydrates: 9g
- Protein: 12g

Ham and Egg Casserole

Serving: 2

Prep Time: 10 minutes

Cook Time: 25 minutes

Ingredients

- 6 whole eggs
- ½ a yellow onion, chopped
- 1 cup ham, chopped
- 1 cup cheddar cheese, shredded
- 4 red potatoes, cubed
- 1 cup milk
- Cooking spray
- 2 cups water
- Pinch of salt and water

How To

1. Take a bowl and add eggs, milk, pepper, salt, potatoes, ham, onion, cheese and whisk well
2. Take a pan and spray with cooking spray
3. Add water to your Instant Pot
4. Add steamer basket inside and add pan
5. Pour egg mixture
6. Close lid and cook on HIGH pressure for 25 minutes
7. Release the pressure naturally over 10 minutes
8. Take the casserole out and slice, divide between 2 plates and enjoy!

Nutrition (Per Serving)

- Calories: 210
- Fat: 2g

- Carbohydrates: 5g
- Protein: 7g

Zucchini Zoodles of Lemon and Parmesan

Serving: 2

Prep Time: 5 minutes

Cook Time: 5 minutes

Ingredients

- 2 tablespoon of olive oil
- 2 garlic cloves, diced
- Zest of ½ a lemon
- ½ a teaspoon of sea flavored vinegar
- 2 large sized zucchini, spiralized or peeled into noodle ribbons
- Juice of ½ a lemon
- 1 tablespoon of mint, sliced
- 4 tablespoon of parmesan, grated
- Cracked black pepper

How To

1. Set your pot to Sauté mode and add olive oil, allow the oil to heat up
2. Add garlic, lemon zest and flavored vinegar and give it a nice stir for 30 seconds
3. Add zucchini noodles and drizzle lemon juice
4. Stir well for 20-30 seconds
5. Sprinkle mint, parmesan over the top and stir
6. Serve and enjoy!

Nutrition (Per Serving)

- Calories: 296
- Fat: 25g
- Carbohydrates: 2g
- Protein: 17g

Early Morning Buckwheat Porridge

Serving: 2

Prep Time: 10 minutes

Cook Time: 6 minutes

Ingredients

- 1 cup buckwheat groats, rinsed
- ½ a cup raisin
- 3 cups rice milk
- 1 banana, peeled and sliced
- ½ a teaspoon of vanilla extract

How To

1. Add buckwheat to your pot
2. Add raisins, milk, banana, vanilla and stir
3. Close lid and cook on HIGH pressure for 6 minutes
4. Release the pressure naturally over 10 minutes
5. Divide porridge between 2 bowls and enjoy!

Nutrition (Per Serving)

- Calories: 162
- Fat: 1g
- Carbohydrates: 2g
- Protein: 5g

Super Blueberry Breakfast

Serving: 2

Prep Time: 5 minutes

Cook Time: 6 minutes

Ingredients

- 2/3 cup old fashioned oats
- 2/3 Greek yogurt
- 2/3 cup almond milk
- 2/3 cup blueberries
- 2 tablespoon chia seeds
- 1 teaspoon of sugar
- A pinch of cinnamon powder
- ½ a teaspoon vanilla
- 1 and a ½ cup water

How To

1. Take a heat-proof bowl and add oats, milk, yogurt, chia seeds, blueberries, sugar, cinnamon and vanilla
2. Stir
3. Add water to your Instant Pot
4. Add trivet and place the bowl
5. Close lid and cook on HIGH pressure for 6 minutes
6. Release pressure naturally over 10 minutes
7. Stir in blueberries and divide between 2 bowls

Nutrition (Per Serving)

- Calories: 154
- Fat: 2g
- Carbohydrates: 2g

Hungry Bear Coffee Oatmeal

Serving: 2

Prep Time: 5 minutes

Cook Time: 3 minutes

Ingredients

For Pot:

- 4 and a ½ cups of water
- 1 and a ½ cups of steel cut oats
- 1 and a ½ cups of pumpkin puree
- 2 teaspoons of cinnamon
- 1 teaspoon of allspice
- 1 teaspoon of vanilla

For Coffee Cake Topping:

- ½ a cup of coconut sugar
- ¼ cup of walnuts
- 1 tablespoon of cinnamon

How To

1. Add all of the listed ingredients to your pot
2. Lock up the lid and cook on HIGH pressure for 3 minutes
3. Take a bowl and add all of the topping ingredients and mix them well
4. Release the pressure naturally once done
5. Serve with the topping and non-dairy milk

Nutrition (Per Serving)

- Calories: 91
- Fat: 2g

- Carbohydrates: 18g
- Protein: 3g

Chapter 6: Appetizer and Snacks Recipes

Red and White Spouts

Serving: 2

Prep Time: 10 minutes

Cook Time: 3 minutes

Ingredients

- 1 pound of Brussels sprouts
- ¼ cup of pine nuts toasted
- 1 pomegranate
- 1 tablespoon of extra virgin olive oil
- ½ a teaspoon of flavored vinegar
- 1 grate pepper

How To

1. Remove the outer leaves and trim the stems
2. Wash the Brussels
3. Cut the largest one in half and get all the ones in uniform size
4. Add 1 cup of water
5. Put steamer basket
6. Add sprouts to steamer basket
7. Lock up the lid and cook on HIGH pressure for 3 minutes
8. Release the pressure naturally
9. Move sprouts to serving dish and dress with olive oil, pepper and flavored vinegar
10. Sprinkle toasted pine nuts and pomegranate seeds
11. Serve and enjoy!

Nutrition (Per Serving)

- Calories: 197

- Fat: 7g
- Carbohydrates: 22g
- Protein: 6g

Off-Beat Chicken Salad

Serving: 2

Prep Time: 5 minutes

Cook Time: 30 minutes

Ingredients

- 1 whole chicken
- 1 cup of water
- 1 cup of sour cream
- 1 teaspoon of garlic powder
- 1 teaspoon of black pepper
- 3 cup of baby spinach
- 3 diced up tomatoes
- 1 sliced up avocado

How To

1. Open lid of your instant pot and pour in water in your inner pot
2. Add in your chicken
3. Close lid and cook for 30 minutes on POULTRY mode
4. While that is being cooked, prepare your salad by taking a bowl and toss in the tomatoes, spinach, avocado and finely mix it
5. Add in your sour cream alongside garlic powder, sprinkled with black pepper
6. By this time, the chicken should be ready. Open up your instant pot and bring it out, only to cut it finely
7. Once cut up, pour in your dressing and serve it warm over your prepared salad

Nutrition (Per Serving)

- Calories: 417
- Fat: 31g
- Carbohydrates: 3g

Classical Rice Porridge

Serving: 2

Prep Time: 5 minutes

Cook Time: 25 minutes

Ingredients

- 1 cup of rice flour
- 1 cup of water
- 1 cup of almond milk
- 3 tablespoon of maple syrup
- 1 tablespoon of coconut oil
- 1 teaspoon of vanilla extract
- 1 cup of cherries, chopped
- 1 cup of almond butter

How To

1. Add all of the listed ingredients to the pot
2. Lock up the lid and cook on HIGH pressure for 2 minutes
3. Release the pressure naturally
4. Serve with a topping of walnuts, maple syrup of anything that you desire (vegan compliant)

Nutrition (Per Serving)

- Calories: 88
- Fat: 0g
- Carbohydrates: 19g
- Protein: 2g

Jar-O-Pickle

Serving: 2

Prep Time: 10 minutes

Cook Time: 11 minutes

Ingredients

- 1 pound of green chilies
- 1 and a ½ cups of apple cider vinegar
- 1 teaspoon of pickling salt
- 1 and a ½ teaspoon of date paste
- ¼ teaspoon of garlic powder

How To

1. Add the above-mentioned ingredients to the pot
2. Lock up the lid and cook on HIGH pressure for 10 minutes
3. Release the pressure naturally
4. Spoon the mix into washed jars and cover the slices with a bit of cooking liquid
5. Add vinegar to submerge the chilly
6. Enjoy!

Nutrition (Per Serving)

- Calories: 4
- Fat: 0g
- Carbohydrates: 0.6g
- Protein: 0.1g

Sautéed Mushroom Curry!

Serving: 2

Prep Time: 3 minutes

Cook Time: 5 minutes

Ingredients

- 16 ounces of mushroom
- 6 garlic cloves, peeled and crushed
- ¼ cup of red wine (vegan compliant)
- 1/2 cup of low sodium vegetable or mushroom stock
- 2 teaspoon of low sodium soy sauce
- Black pepper as required
- 1 tablespoon of browning sauce

How To

1. Add the ingredients to the pot
2. Lock up the lid and cook on HIGH pressure for 4 minutes
3. Quick release the pressure
4. If the consistency of the sauce is ok, then serve
5. Otherwise, set the pot to Sauté mode and allow the sauce to reach boiling point
6. Take a bowl and add ¼ cup of water and 2-3 tablespoon of cornstarch
7. Pour the slurry into the liquid while it is boiling and stir
8. Serve over potato or rice

Nutrition (Per Serving)

- Calories: 486
- Fat: 7g
- Carbohydrates: 71g
- Protein: 37g

Chapter 7: Beef, Lamb and Pork Recipes

Cool Beef Bourguignon

Serving: 2

Prep Time: 10 minutes

Cook Time: 50 minutes

<u>Ingredients</u>

- ½ pound beef stew meat
- 2 bacon slices
- 1 garlic clove, minced
- 1 medium onion, chopped
- 2 medium carrots, chopped
- 1 tablespoon parsley
- 1 tablespoon of thyme
- ½ a cup beef stock
- ½ cup red wine
- 1 large potato, cubed
- ½ a tablespoon of honey
- ½ a tablespoon olive oil

<u>How To</u>

1. Set your pot to Sauté mode
2. Add oil and allow the oil to heat up
3. Add beef and cook for 3-4 minutes
4. Keep the beef on the side
5. Add bacon and onion and Sauté until onions are translucent
6. Add beef and the remaining ingredients
7. Lock up the lid and cook on HIGH pressure for 30 minutes
8. Release pressure naturally over 10 minutes

9. Serve and enjoy!

<u>Nutrition (Per Serving)</u>

- Calories: 559
- Fat: 17g
- Carbohydrates: 47g
- Protein: 43g

Dramatically Simple Lasagna

Serving: 2

Prep Time: 2 minutes

Cook Time: 10 minutes

Ingredients

- 6-ounce ruffles pasta
- 4 ounces ricotta cheese
- 4 ounces mozzarella cheese
- ¼ pound ground beef
- ¼ pound ground pork
- 1 cup pasta sauce
- 1 cup water

How To

1. Set your pot to Sauté mode and add beef and pork, cook until crumbly
2. Add water, pasta and sauce
3. Close lid and cook on HIGH pressure for 5 minutes
4. Perform quick release
5. Add ricotta cheese, half of mozzarella and stir
6. Serve hot with a topping of remaining mozzarella
7. Enjoy!

Nutrition (Per Serving)

- Calories: 691
- Fat: 24g
- Carbohydrates: 52g
- Protein: 62g

Instant Picadillo

Serving: 2

Prep Time: 10 minutes

Cook Time: 15 minutes

Ingredients

- ¾ pound ground beef
- ½ large onion, chopped
- 1 tomato, chopped
- 1 garlic clove, minced
- 1 bay leaf
- 2 ounces tomato sauce
- 1 tablespoon olives, pitted
- 1 tablespoon cilantro, chopped
- ½ cup water

How To

1. Set pot to Sauté mode and add beef, break meat into pieces and cook until browned
2. Add the remaining ingredients and mix
3. Close lid and cook on HIGH pressure for 15 minutes
4. Perform quick release
5. Serve with salad or rice
6. Enjoy!

Nutrition (Per Serving)

- Calories: 352
- Fat: 11g
- Carbohydrates: 7g
- Protein: 52g

Two People Parmesan Honey Pork Roast

Serving: 2

Prep Time: 5 minutes

Cook Time: 35 minutes

Ingredients

- 1-pound pork roast
- 2 tablespoon parmesan cheese, grated
- 1 tablespoon soy sauce
- ½ a tablespoon dry basil
- ½ a tablespoon of garlic, minced
- ½ a tablespoon olive oil
- Salt as needed
- ½ tablespoon of corn starch
- ½ cup water

How To

1. Add the listed ingredients to your Instant Pot
2. Lock lid and cook on MEAT/STEW mode and set timer to 35 minutes
3. Release the pressure naturally over 10 minutes
4. Serve and enjoy!

Nutrition (Per Serving)

- Calories: 653
- Fat: 29g
- Carbohydrates: 20g
- Protein: 71g

Carne Guisada From Mexico

Serving: 2

Prep Time: 10 minutes

Cook Time: 3 minutes

Ingredients

- 3 pound of beef stew
- 3 tablespoons of seasoned salt
- 1 tablespoon of oregano chili powder
- 1 tablespoon organic cumin
- 1 pinch of crushed red pepper
- 2 tablespoon of olive oil
- ½ of a medium lime, juiced
- 1 cup of beef bone broth
- 3 ounce of tomato paste
- 1 large onion, thinly sliced up

How To

1. Trim the beef stew as needed into small bite sized portions
2. Add the beef stew pieces with dry seasoning
3. Set your pot to Sauté mode and add oil, allow the oil to heat up
4. Add seasoned beef pieces and brown them
5. Combine the browned beef pieces with rest of the ingredients
6. Lock up the lid and cook on HIGH pressure for 3 minutes
7. Release the pressure naturally
8. Enjoy!

Nutrition (Per Serving)

- Calories: 274
- Fat: 12g

- Carbohydrates: 11g
- Protein: 33g

Chapter 8: Poultry Recipes

Sweetest Potato Chicken Curry

Serving: 2

Prep Time: 10 minutes

Cook Time: 17 minutes

<u>Ingredients</u>

- 1 tablespoon coconut oil
- 1 tablespoon curry powder
- 1 teaspoon of ground turmeric
- 1 teaspoon cumin
- ½ a teaspoon of salt
- ½ a teaspoon of cayenne pepper
- ¼ medium yellow onion, diced
- 1 cup green beans
- 2 garlic cloves, minced
- 1 red pepper, diced
- ½ chicken breast, cubed
- ¼ cup chicken broth
- 1 sweet potato, cubed
- 1 tablespoon of fresh cilantro, chopped

<u>How To</u>

1. Set your pot to Sauté mode and add garlic, onion, oil and Sauté until onion color changes

2. Add sweet potatoes, chicken, red pepper, green beans, curry, cumin, broth, salt and turmeric

3. Close lid and cook on HIGH pressure for 12 minutes

4. Perform a quick release

5. Serve with garnish of cilantro

6. Enjoy!

<u>Nutrition (Per Serving)</u>

- Calories: 295
- Fat: 10g
- Carbohydrates: 25g
- Protein: 25g

Ultimate Chicken Wings

Serving: 2

Prep Time: 15 minutes

Cook Time: 15 minutes

Ingredients

- 1 and ½ pound chicken wings
- ¼ cup tomato puree
- 1 tablespoon honey
- 1 tablespoon fresh lemon juice
- Salt and pepper as needed

How To

1. Arrange steamer trivet in your Instant Pot
2. Add a cup of water
3. Place chicken wings on top
4. Lock up the lid and cook on HIGH pressure for 10 minutes
5. Perform quick release
6. Pre-heat your broiler
7. Take a bowl and add remaining ingredients and beat until combined
8. Transfer chicken wings to sauce bowl
9. Coat wings with sauce
10. Arrange chicken wings on parchment paper lined baking sheet
11. Broiler for 5 minutes

Nutrition (Per Serving)

- Calories: 692
- Fat: 25g
- Carbohydrates: 11g
- Protein: 99g

Roasted Cornish Hen

Serving: 2

Prep Time: 20 minutes

Cook Time: 19 minutes

Ingredients

- 1 Cornish hen
- Salt and pepper
- 1 tablespoon of olive oil
- 1 small onion, chopped
- 1 celery stalk, chopped
- 1 medium carrot, peeled and chopped
- 2 garlic cloves, chopped
- 1 teaspoon of Worcestershire sauce
- ¾ cup water

How To

1. Wash the hen and dry with paper towel
2. Rub salt and pepper hen all over
3. Set the pot to Sauté mode and add oil, allow the oil to heat up
4. Add hen and Sauté for 2 minutes per side
5. Add rest of the ingredients
6. Lock up lid and cook on HIGH pressure for 15 minutes
7. Release pressure naturally over 10 minutes
8. Transfer hen onto platter and cool for 5 minutes
9. Serve with veggies
10. Enjoy!

Nutrition (Per Serving)

- Calories: 267

- Fat: 12g
- Carbohydrates: 8g
- Protein: 30g

Ingenious Chicken Cacciatore

Serving: 2

Prep Time: 5 minutes

Cook Time: 15 minutes

Ingredients

- 6 chicken thighs
- 1 large yellow onion, chopped
- 1 cup chicken broth
- 1 bay leaf
- 1 teaspoon of garlic powder
- 1 teaspoon oregano
- ¾ cup black olives
- ¼ teaspoon of salt
- 6 medium tomatoes, chopped

How To

1. Add the listed ingredients to your Instant Pot except olives
2. Close lid and cook on HIGH pressure for 15 minutes
3. Release the pressure naturally over 10 minutes
4. Open lid and garnish with olives
5. Serve and enjoy!

Nutrition (Per Serving)

- Calories: 327
- Fat: 18g
- Carbohydrates: 13g
- Protein: 27g

Cajun Chicken Fried Rice

Serving: 2

Prep Time: 10 minutes

Cook Time: 15 minutes

Ingredients

- ½ pound chicken breast, cubed
- ½ tablespoon Cajun seasoning
- ½ tablespoon of olive oil
- ½ onion, diced
- 1 garlic clove, minced
- ½ tablespoon tomato paste
- ¾ cups white rice rinsed
- 1 red bell pepper, diced
- 1 cup vegetable broth

How To

1. Set your pot to Sauté mode and add oil, allow the oil to heat up
2. Add garlic and onion and cook until browned
3. Press Cancel and add chicken breast, tomato paste, Cajun seasoning, rice, bell pepper, vegetable broth
4. Stir well
5. Close lid and cook on HIGH pressure for 10 minutes
6. Perform a natural pressure release over 10 minutes
7. Open lid and stir
8. Enjoy!

Nutrition (Per Serving)

- Calories: 470
- Fat: 8g

- Carbohydrates: 65g
- Protein: 32g

Butter Chicken Delight

Serving: 2

Prep Time: 10 minutes

Cook Time: 12 minutes

Ingredients

- 2 chicken thigh, boneless and skinless, cubed
- ½ a cup heavy cream
- 1 tablespoon onion, cubed
- ½ a tablespoon of garlic, minced
- ½ a tablespoon of ginger, minced
- ½ a teaspoon of chili powder
- ½ a teaspoon of cumin
- ¼ teaspoon salt
- ½ a cup water

How To

1. Set your pot to Sauté mode and add butter
2. Add chicken and onion and cook until the chicken is slightly brown
3. Add the remaining ingredients and close lid
4. Cook on HIGH pressure for 8 minutes
5. Release naturally over 10 minutes
6. Serve warm!

Nutrition (Per Serving)

- Calories: 479
- Fat: 32g
- Carbohydrates: 4g
- Protein: 45g

Ecstatic Duck Breast

Serving: 2

Prep Time: 2 hours

Cook Time: 30 minutes

Ingredients

- 2 halves of duck breast, boneless skin on
- 1 teaspoon of salt
- 2 teaspoons of freshly minced garlic
- ½ a teaspoon of black pepper
- 1/3 teaspoon of thyme
- 1/3 teaspoon of peppercorn
- 1 tablespoon of olive oil
- 1 tablespoon apricot, peeled and cored
- 2 teaspoon of date paste

How To

1. Clean the duck breast and rub the ingredients all over
2. Cover and allow it to chill for 2 hours
3. Rinse the spices off and place the breast in a zip bag, seal it up making sure to remove as much air as possible. (look on the internet for immersion sealing method for best results)
4. Add water to your pot Up to the 7-cup mark
5. Set your pot to Sauté mode and allow the water to heat up for about 20 minutes
6. Place the bag in the water bath and keep it for 35-40 minutes
7. Remove the bag from water and pat the breasts dry
8. Sear the skin side of the duck breast in a nonstick frying pan with about 1 tablespoon of oil over medium-high heat
9. Turn the breast over and cook for 20 seconds more

10. Prepare the apricot sauce by mixing apricot and date paste in a small pot and bringing the mix to a boil, followed by a simmer for 5 minutes at low heat
11. Slice the duck breast and serve with apricot sauce
12. Serve the duck breast with the sauce
13. Enjoy!

<u>Nutrition (Per Serving)</u>

- Calories: 306
- Fats: 19g
- Carbs:8g
- Protein:17g

Chapter 9: Fish and Seafood Recipes

Salmon Chili Lime Sauce

Serving: 2

Prep Time: 10 minutes

Cook Time: 5 minutes

Ingredients

For Steaming Salmon

- 2 pieces of salmon fillets of 5 ounce each
- 1 cup of water
- Freshly ground black pepper

For Chili-Lime Sauce

- 1 jalapeno, seeded and diced
- 1 juice lime
- 2 minced garlic cloves
- 1 tablespoon honey
- 1 tablespoon olive oil
- 1 tablespoon hot water
- 1 tablespoon fresh parsley, chopped
- ½ a teaspoon paprika
- ½ a teaspoon cumin

How To

1. Add the listed ingredients to a bowl and mix, keep it on the side
2. Add water to the Instant Pot
3. Place salmon fillets on a steam rack and place it inside your pot
4. Season with pepper

5. Lock up the lid and cook on HIGH pressure for 5 minutes
6. Release the pressure naturally over 10 minutes
7. Open and serve with a drizzle of chili-lime sauce
8. Enjoy!

<u>Nutrition (Per Serving)</u>

- Calories: 444
- Fat: 23g
- Carbohydrates: 18g
- Protein: 38g

Tender Steamed Salmon Fillets

Serving: 2

Prep Time: 10 minutes

Cook Time: 5 minutes

Ingredients

- 2 salmon fillets
- ¼ cup of chopped up onion
- 2 stalks green onion, chopped
- 1 egg
- Almond meal as needed
- Salt as needed
- Pepper as needed
- 2 tablespoon of olive oil

How To

1. Add a cup of water to your pot and place a steamer rack on top
2. Place the fish
3. Season the fish with salt and pepper and lock up the lid
4. Cook on HIGH pressure for 3 minutes
5. Once done, quick release the pressure
6. Remove the fish and allow it to cool
7. Break the fillets into a bowl and add egg, yellow and green onions
8. Add ½ a cup of almond meal and mix with your hand
9. Divide the mixture into patties
10. Take a large skillet and place it over medium heat
11. Add oil and cook the patties
12. Enjoy!

Nutrition (Per Serving)

- Calories: 238
- Fat: 15g
- Carbohydrates: 1g
- Protein: 23g

Fancy Glazed Salmon

Serving: 2

Prep Time: 15 minutes

Cook Time: 5 minutes

Ingredients

- 2 salmon fillets
- Salt and pepper to taste
- 1 jalapeno pepper, seeded and chopped
- 2 garlic cloves, minced
- 1 tablespoon fresh parsley, chopped
- 2 tablespoon fresh lime juice
- 1 tablespoon olive oil
- 1 tablespoon honey
- 1 tablespoon hot water
- ½ a teaspoon ground cumin
- ½ a teaspoon paprika

How To

1. Season the salmon fillets with pepper and salt
2. Take a bowl and add the rest of the ingredients to make the sauce
3. Place steamer trivet in your Pot and add a cup of water
4. Place salmon fillet on top of trivet
5. Lock lid and cook on STEAM mode for 5 minutes
6. Perform a quick release
7. Remove lid and transfer salmon to serving plates
8. Drizzle sauce and enjoy!

Nutrition (Per Serving)

- Calories: 290

- Fat: 16g
- Carbohydrates: 10g
- Protein: 28g

Juicy Mediterranean Calamari

Serving: 2

Prep Time: 10 minutes

Cook Time: 4 minutes

Ingredients

- 1-pound calamari, chopped
- 1 tablespoon olive oil
- ½ red onion, sliced
- 1 garlic clove, chopped
- ½ a cup of red wine
- 1 celery stalk, chopped
- 1 cup tomatoes, crushed
- 1 sprig fresh rosemary
- 2 tablespoon Italian parsley, chopped
- Salt and pepper as needed

How To

1. Toss calamari pieces in olive oil and season with salt and pepper
2. Add wine, celery, tomatoes, rosemary, red onion and garlic to your Instant Pot
3. Add calamari in a steamer basket and lower into the liquid
4. Close lid and cook on HIGH pressure for 4 minutes
5. Perform quick release
6. Remove fish and sprinkle fresh parsley

Nutrition (Per Serving)

- Calories: 332
- Fat: 10g
- Carbohydrates: 12g
- Protein: 35g

Slightly Spicy Shrimp Meal

Serving: 2

Prep Time: 10 minutes

Cook Time: 5 minutes

Ingredients

- 1-pound frozen shrimp, peeled and deveined
- 1 lemon, juiced
- 1 teaspoon black pepper
- 1 teaspoon of white pepper
- 1 teaspoon of cayenne pepper
- 1 can diced tomatoes (14-15 ounces)
- 1 jalapeno pepper, minced
- 2 garlic cloves, minced
- 1 sweet onion, minced

How To

1. Pour tomatoes and juices to your Instant Pot
2. Add lemon juice, onion and garlic and stir
3. Let the frozen shrimp come to room temp and add to your pot
4. Add jalapeno
5. Add black, white and cayenne pepper
6. Mix and close lid
7. Cook on HIGH pressure for 5 minutes
8. Perform quick release and serve!

Nutrition (Per Serving)

- Calories: 174
- Fat: 2.3g
- Carbohydrates: 10g

Perfectly Steamed Mussels

Serving: 2

Prep Time: 10 minutes

Cook Time: 3 minutes

Ingredients

- 2-pound fresh mussels, cleaned and rinsed
- 1 cup tomatoes, diced
- ½ cup white wine
- ½ a tablespoon of pepper
- ½ a tablespoon of dried parsley
- Salt as needed

How To

1. Pour tomato into your Instant Pot alongside juices
2. Add wine
3. Stir and season with salt and pepper
4. Add parsley
5. Place mussels in steamer basket and lower into liquid
6. Close lid and cook on HIGH pressure for 3 minutes
7. Perform quick release
8. Remove lid and cover mussels with the sauce
9. Serve and enjoy!

Nutrition (Per Serving)

- Calories: 460
- Fat: 10g
- Carbohydrates: 22g
- Protein: 55g

Parsley and Peas with Cod

Serving: 2

Prep Time: 5 minutes

Cook Time: 5 minutes

Ingredients

- 2-pound cod, cut into 2 fillets
- 5-ounce frozen peas
- ½ cup fresh parsley
- ½ cup white wine
- 1 garlic clove, smashed
- ½ teaspoon of paprika
- ½ teaspoon of oregano
- 1 sprig fresh rosemary
- Salt and pepper as needed

How To

1. Take a bowl and add wine, salt, herbs and spices
2. Stir well
3. Pour liquid into Instant Pot and add frozen peas
4. Place fish into steamer basket, lower into liquid
5. Close lid and cook on HIGH pressure for 5 minutes
6. Quick release pressure
7. Serve by transferring the peas to a platter and placing the fish on top

Nutrition (Per Serving)

- Calories: 234
- Fat: 1.4g
- Carbohydrates: 13g
- Protein: 30g

Seafood Stew for The Ages

Serving: 2

Prep Time: 10 minutes

Cook Time: 10 minutes

<u>Ingredients</u>

- 4 tablespoon extra-virgin olive oil
- 2 bay leaves
- 2 teaspoons paprika
- 1 small onion, thinly sliced
- 1 green bell pepper, thinly sliced
- 2 cloves garlic, smashed
- Salt and pepper as needed
- 1 cup fish stock
- 1 and a ½ pound meaty fish
- 1-pound shrimp, cleaned and deveined
- 12 little neck clams
- ¼ cup cilantro for garnish

<u>How To</u>

1. Set your pot to Sauté mode and add olive oil
2. Add bay leaves and paprika and Sauté for 30 seconds
3. Add onion, bell pepper, tomatoes, 2 tablespoons of cilantro, garlic and season with salt and pepper
4. Stir for a few minutes
5. Add fish stock
6. Season fish with salt and pepper and Nestle the clams and shrimp among the veggies in the pot
7. Add fish on top
8. Lock up the lid and cook on HIGH pressure for 10 minutes

9. Release the pressure over 10 minutes
10. Divide the stew amongst bowls and drizzle 1 tablespoon of olive oil
11. Sprinkle 2 tablespoon of cilantro and serve
12. Enjoy!

Nutrition (Per Serving)

- Calories: 401
- Fat: 20g
- Carbohydrates: 9g
- Protein: 41g

Tender Steamed Salmon Fillets

Serving: 2

Prep Time: 10 minutes

Cook Time: 5 minutes

<u>Ingredients</u>

- 1 pound of tilapia fillets cut up in 2-inch pieces
- 1 tablespoon of olive oil
- ½ a teaspoon of mustard seed
- 1 can of coconut milk
- 1 tablespoon of ginger garlic paste
- 10-15 pieces of curry leaves
- ½ of a medium onion, sliced
- ½ of a green pepper, sliced
- ½ of a yellow pepper, sliced
- 1 teaspoon of salt
- ½ a teaspoon of turmeric powder
- ½ a teaspoon of red chili powder
- 2 teaspoon of coriander powder
- 1 teaspoon of cumin powder
- ½ a teaspoon of Garam Masala
- 2-3 sprigs of cilantro
- 6-8 mint leaves
- ½ a teaspoon of lime juice

<u>How To</u>

1. Cut up the tilapia into 2-inch pieces
2. Slice the onion and bell pepper and add the chopped ginger-garlic
3. Mix well to prepare the paste
4. Set your pot to Sauté mode and add olive oil, allow the oil to heat up

5. Add mustard seed and allow them to splutter
6. Add curry leaves, ginger, garlic paste and Sauté for 30 seconds
7. Add sliced onion, bell pepper and Sauté for 30 seconds more
8. Add spices and stir for 30 seconds
9. Add coconut milk and simmer for 30 seconds
10. Add tilapia (cut up into 2-inch pieces) alongside a few cilantro sprigs and stir well to coat them up with the coconut milk
11. Add a few minute leaves on top
12. Lock up the lid and cook on HIGH pressure for 2-3 minutes
13. Do a quick release and serve!

Nutrition (Per Serving)

- Calories: 392
- Fat: 27g
- Carbohydrates: 12g
- Protein: 29g

Chapter 10: Rice, Beans and Grains Recipes

Quick Breakfast Oatmeal

Serving: 2

Prep Time: 10 minutes

Cook Time: 3 minutes

Ingredients

- ½ a cup steel cut oat
- 1 and a ½ cups water
- 1 teaspoon of vanilla extract

How To

1. Add water to your Instant Pot
2. Add vanilla extract, oats and stir
3. Close lid and cook on HIGH pressure for 3 minutes
4. Release the pressure naturally over 10 minutes
5. Open and divide between 2 bowls
6. Enjoy!

Nutrition (Per Serving)

- Calories: 142
- Fat: 1g
- Carbohydrates: 2g
- Protein: 2g

Early Morning Quinoa Breakfast

Serving: 2

Prep Time: 10 minutes

Cook Time: 1 minute

Ingredients

- 1 cup quinoa
- 2 cups water
- 1 tablespoon of maple syrup
- ¼ teaspoon of vanilla extract
- Pinch of cinnamon powder
- ¼ cup fresh berries

How To

1. Add quinoa to your Instant Pot
2. Add cinnamon, vanilla, water and maple syrup
3. Stir and close lid
4. Cook on HIGH pressure for 1 minute
5. Release the pressure naturally over 10 minutes
6. Open lid and fluff with fork
7. Divide between 2 bowls and top with fresh berries
8. Serve and enjoy!

Nutrition (Per Serving)

- Calories: 173
- Fat: 1g
- Carbohydrates: 2g
- Protein: 3g

Authentic Black Bean Rice

Serving: 2

Prep Time: 10 minutes

Cook Time: 45 minutes

Ingredients

- 1 cup of brown rice
- ½ a cup of dry black beans
- 2 and a ½ cup of water
- ½ a medium red onion, diced
- ½ red pepper, diced
- 2 garlic cloves, minced
- 1 teaspoon of better than bouillon cubes
- 1 tablespoon of chili powder
- ½ a teaspoon of cayenne pepper
- 1 teaspoon of cumin

How To

1. Mince garlic
2. Dice the onions
3. Set your pot to Sauté mode and add the garlic and onions, Sauté for 5 minutes
4. Set your pot to WARM mode and add the remaining ingredients (Except pepper)
5. Lock up the lid and cook on HIGH pressure for 25 minutes
6. Release the pressure naturally over 10 minutes
7. Add diced red pepper and serve!

Nutrition (Per Serving)

- Calories: 190
- Fat: 1g
- Carbohydrates: 39g

Ultimate Gluten Free Mushroom Risotto

Serving: 2

Prep Time: 5 minutes

Cook Time: 10 minutes

Ingredients

- ½ a cup of white onion, minced
- 3 cloves garlic, minced
- 1 tablespoon of olive oil
- 4 ounce of mushrooms, chopped up and broken into small pieces
- 1 teaspoon of salt
- 1 teaspoon of thyme
- ½ a cup of dry white wine
- 3 cups of vegetable broth
- 1 cup of Arborio Rice
- ¼ cup of lemon juice
- 2 cups of fresh spinach
- 1 tablespoon of vegan butter
- 1 and an extra ½ tablespoon of nutritional yeast
- Black pepper as needed

How To

1. Set your pot to Sauté mode and add olive oil
2. Heat it up and add garlic and onions, Sauté them for about 3 minutes
3. Add rice and stir finely
4. Add broth, wine, thyme, salt and mushrooms
5. Lock up the lid and let it cook at high pressure for 5 minutes
6. Carefully quick release the pressure and open up the lid
7. Stir in some spinach, vegan butter, black pepper and nutritional yeast
8. Stir for a few minutes

9. Serve once cool and thick

Nutrition (Per Serving)

- Calories: 312
- Fat: 17g
- Carbohydrates: 32g
- Protein: 5g

Kidney and Lentil Bean Delight

Serving: 2

Prep Time: 10 minutes

Cook Time: 10 minutes

Ingredients

- ½ a cup of dry brown lentils
- 1 cup of cooked kidney beans
- 2 teaspoons of oil
- ½ of red onion, chopped
- 1 green chili, chopped
- 2-3 garlic cloves, chopped
- 2 medium tomatoes, chopped
- ½ a teaspoon of chipotle pepper powder
- 2-3 teaspoon of special spice blend (given below)
- ½ red bell pepper, chopped
- ¼ celery, chopped
- 2 cups of water
- ¾ teaspoon of flavored vinegar
- ½ a cup of fresh corn
- Lemon juice, sour cream, yogurt, cilantro for garnish

Spice Mix

- 1 tablespoon of cayenne pepper
- 1 teaspoon of garlic granules
- ½ a teaspoon of onion powder
- 2 teaspoon of cumin powder
- 1-2 teaspoon of smoked paprika
- ½ a teaspoon of oregano
- ½ a teaspoon of coriander powder

- ¼ teaspoon of black pepper

How To

1. Take a bowl and add everything listed under spices and mix well
2. Wash the lentils thoroughly and drain them, keep them on the side
3. Set your pot to Sauté mode and add oil, allow the oil to heat up
4. Add onion and Sauté for 4 minutes
5. Add green chili pepper, garlic and cook for 2 minutes more
6. Add chipotle pepper, tomatoes, spice and cook for 5 minutes until the tomatoes are saucy
7. Add bell pepper and celery and stir well
8. Cook for 1 minute
9. Add lentil, kidney beans, corn, flavored vinegar and a cup of water
10. Lock up the lid and cook on HIGH pressure for 7-9 minutes
11. Release the pressure naturally over 10 minutes
12. Garnish and serve!

Nutrition (Per Serving)

- Calories: 312
- Fat: 5g
- Carbohydrates: 61g
- Protein: 8g

Generous Vegan Chili

Serving: 2

Prep Time: 7 minutes

Cook Time: 30 minutes

Ingredients

- 2 tablespoon of vegetable oil
- 1 large sized diced onion
- 5 garlic clove, minced
- 6 cups of tomato juice
- 1 cup of water
- 1 tablespoon + an extra 1 teaspoon of chili powder
- 1 teaspoon of garlic powder
- ½ a teaspoon of cumin
- 1 teaspoon of sea flavored vinegar
- Dash of pepper
- 7 cups of canned or soaked kidney beans
- 2 cans of tomatoes, diced

How To

1. Set your Instant Pot to Sauté mode and add onions
2. Sauté for a while and add garlic, and Sauté for 1 minute
3. Add spices and stir in your tomato juice
4. Use an immersion blender to blend until you have a sauce like mixture
5. Add the remaining ingredients
6. Lock up the lid and cook on HIGH pressure for 7 minutes
7. Release the pressure naturally over 10 minutes and serve!

Nutrition (Per Serving)

- Calories: 194

- Fat: 6g
- Carbohydrates: 29g
- Protein: 10g

Asparagus Risotto with Micro stock

Serving: 2

Prep Time: 10 minutes

Cook Time: 10 minutes

Ingredients

- 1 pound of asparagus
- 4 cups of water
- 2 tablespoon of olive oil
- 1 medium red onion, chopped
- 2 cups of Arborio rice
- ¼ cup of white wine vinegar
- 2 teaspoons of flavored vinegar
- ½ a teaspoon of lemon juice

How To

1. Trim the asparagus by removing the stem, wash them under cold water and slice them in rondels making sure to keep the tips
2. Add woody stems and water to your Instant Pot
3. Lock up the lid and cook on HIGH pressure for 12 minutes, release the pressure naturally
4. Lift out the woody stem and discard the cooking liquid
5. Pour the liquid into a measuring cup
6. Add onion, olive oil to the pot and swirl
7. Add rice, onion and stir
8. Cook for 2 minutes
9. Splash in a bit of wine vinegar and deglaze
10. Add asparagus micro stock, asparagus rondels and tips
11. Season with flavored vinegar
12. Lock up the lid and cook on HIGH pressure for 6 minutes

13. Release the pressure naturally
14. Add a squeeze of lemon juice and serve
15. Enjoy!

<u>Nutrition (Per Serving)</u>

- Calories: 486
- Fat: 7g
- Carbohydrates: 71g
- Protein: 37g

Perfect Asian Quinoa

Serving: 2

Prep Time: 5 minutes

Cook Time: 10 minutes

Ingredients

- 2 cups of quinoa
- 4 cups of water
- 2 tablespoon of soy sauce
- 2 tablespoon of rice vinegar
- 2 tablespoons of sugar
- 1 thumb of grated ginger
- 8-ounce bag of frozen mixed vegetables

How To

1. Take the veggies out from the fridge and thaw them
2. Add the listed ingredients to the pot (except veggies)
3. Lock up the lid and cook on HIGH pressure for 1 minute
4. Naturally release the pressure
5. Open the lid and add thawed vegetables
6. Stir and serve!

Nutrition (Per Serving)

- Calories: 249
- Fat: 12g
- Carbohydrates: 25g
- Protein: 12g

Chapter 11: Vegetables Recipes

Veggie Khichdi

Serving: 2

Prep Time: 10 minutes

Cook Time: 27 minutes

Ingredients

- 2 tablespoon coconut oil
- 1 teaspoon cumin seed
- 1 tablespoon Ginger
- 1 whole carrot, peeled and sliced
- ¼ cup green beans, chopped
- ¼ cup of frozen green peas
- 1 red potatoes, cubed
- 1 tomatoes, diced
- 1 cup cauliflower, chopped
- 1 cup cabbage, chopped
- 1 cup spinach, chopped
- ½ a teaspoon of turmeric
- 2 teaspoon of mild red chili powder
- 2 teaspoons of flavored vinegar
- 1 cup of white rice
- 1 cup of mixed lentils
- 6 cups of water
- ¼ cup chopped cilantro

How To

1. Set your pot to Sauté mode and add oil, cumin seeds and ginger
2. Cook for 30 seconds

3. Add vegetables and mix well
4. Add red chili powder, flavored vinegar, turmeric and mix
5. Add rice and lentils
6. Add 6 cups of water and stir
7. Lock up the lid and cook on RICE settings for 12 minutes
8. Release the pressure naturally over 10 minutes
9. Serve with roasted pickles/poppadum and enjoy!

Nutrition (Per Serving)

- Calories: 703
- Fat: 15g
- Carbohydrates: 122g
- Protein: 123g

Amazing Red Coconut Curry

Serving: 2

Prep Time: 5 minutes

Cook Time: 15 minutes

Ingredients

- ¾ cup of chickpeas
- 8 ounce of white mushroom, sliced up
- 1 onion, diced
- 2 garlic cloves, minced
- 1 green chili, seeded and diced
- 1 tablespoon of ginger
- ½ a tablespoon of turmeric
- 1 can of coconut milk
- ½ a cup of vegetable stock
- 3 tablespoon of red curry paste
- ½ a tablespoon of salt
- 1 teaspoon of cumin
- ½ a teaspoon of curry powder
- ¼ teaspoon of ground fenugreek
- ¼ teaspoon of black pepper
- 1 tablespoon of tomato paste
- 1-2 teaspoon of lemon juice
- 1 cup of spinach

How To

1. Set the pot to Sauté mode and add mushrooms to the inner pot
2. Cook mushroom until they reduce in size
3. Add onion and Stir well
4. Cook until tender

5. Add chili, garlic, ginger, turmeric and Sauté for 1-2 minutes
6. Add the rest of the ingredients and add coconut milk
7. Add black pepper and Cancel Sauté mode
8. Lock up the lid and cook on HIGH pressure for 15 minutes
9. Release the pressure naturally
10. Stir in tomato paste, spinach and lemon juice
11. Enjoy!

<u>Nutrition (Per Serving)</u>

- Calories: 491
- Fat: 12g
- Carbohydrates: 27g
- Protein: 69g

Lovely Artichoke Delight

Serving: 2

Prep Time: 10 minutes

Cook Time: 27 minutes

Ingredients

- 2 whole artichokes
- 3 whole lemon
- 2 cloves garlic, peeled and sliced
- 3 tablespoon olive oil
- Flavored vinegar
- Black pepper

How To

1. Wash your artichokes well and dip them in water
2. Cut ½ inch from the top
3. Cut the stem to about ½ inch long
4. Trim the thorny tips and outer leaves and rub the chokes with lemon
5. Poke garlic slivers between the choke leaves
6. Place a trivet basket in the Instant Pot and add your Artichokes
7. Lock up the lid and cook on HIGH pressure for 7 minutes
8. Release the pressure naturally over 10 minutes
9. Transfer the artichokes to cutting board and allow them to cool
10. Cut them half lengthwise and cut the purple white center
11. Pre-heat your oven to 400-degree Fahrenheit
12. Take a bowl and mix 1 and ½ lemon and olive oil
13. Pour over the choke halves and sprinkle flavored vinegar and pepper
14. Place an iron skillet in your oven and heat it up for 5 minutes
15. Add a few teaspoons of oil and place the marinated artichoke halves in the skillet
16. Brush with lemon and olive oil mixture

17. Cut third lemon in quarter and nestle them between the halves
18. Roast for 20-25 minutes until the chokes are browned
19. Serve and enjoy!

Nutrition (Per Serving)

- Calories: 263
- Fat: 16g
- Carbohydrates: 8g
- Protein: 23g

Authentic Italian Vegie Platter

Serving: 2

Prep Time: 45 minutes

Cook Time: 10 minutes

Ingredients

- 1 large eggplant, cubed
- 1 teaspoon of slat
- ¼ cup of olive oil
- 1 medium sized pepped, cut up into strips red/yellow strips
- 2 medium sized zucchini, cut up into rounds
- 2 medium sized potatoes, cubed
- 10 cherry tomatoes, halved
- 1 tablespoon of Capers
- 2 tablespoon of pine nuts
- 1 tablespoon of raisins
- ¼ cup of raisins
- 1 bunch of chopped basil
- Flavored vinegar as needed
- Pepper as needed

How To

1. Add eggplant cubes to a strainer and sprinkle a bit of flavored vinegar
2. Allow them to purge for 30 minutes
3. Set your pot to Sauté mode and add olive oil, allow the oil to heat up
4. Add potatoes, eggplant and cook for 3 minutes
5. Add pepper, onion and Sauté for 3 minutes more
6. Add zucchini and cook for 3 minutes
7. Add half of the pine nuts, chopped up basil, raisins, olives, pepper, flavored vinegar
8. Lock up the lid and cook on HIGH pressure for 6 minutes

9. Perform a quick release
10. Transfer the contents to a pot and serve
11. Enjoy!

Nutrition (Per Serving)

- Calories: 155
- Fat: 9g
- Carbohydrates: 17g
- Protein: 3g

Healthy Daikon Bowl

Serving: 2

Prep Time: 10 minutes

Cook Time: 15 minutes

Ingredients

- 2 tablespoon of coconut oil
- 1 pound of boneless and skinless chicken thigh
- 1 cup celery, diced
- 1 cup carrots, diced
- ¾ cup green onion, chopped
- 6 cups of chicken stock
- ½ a teaspoon of dried basil
- 1 teaspoon of sea flavored vinegar
- 1/6 teaspoon of fresh ground pepper
- 2 cups of Spiralized daikon noodles

How To

1. Set your pot to Sauté mode and add coconut oil
2. Allow the oil to heat up and add the chicken thigh
3. Sauté for about 10 minutes
4. Take the chicken out and shred it up
5. Add carrots, onion to the pot and cook for 2 minutes more
6. Add the rest of the ingredients and lock up the lid
7. Cook on HIGH pressure for 15 minutes and quick release
8. Transfer the shredded chicken back to the noodle and stir
9. Enjoy!

Nutrition (Per Serving)

- Calories: 185

- Fat: 5g
- Carbohydrates: 5g
- Protein: 10g

Cool Jackfruit Dish

Serving: 2

Prep Time: 10 minutes

Cook Time: 10 minutes

<u>Ingredients</u>

- 1 teaspoon of oil
- ½ a teaspoon of cumin seeds
- ½ a teaspoon of mustard seeds
- ½ a teaspoon of nigella seeds
- 2 pieces of bay leaves
- 2 dried red chilies
- 1 small onion, chopped
- 5 garlic cloves, chopped
- 1-inch ginger, chopped
- 1 teaspoon of coriander powder
- ½ a teaspoon of turmeric
- ¼ teaspoon of black pepper
- 2 medium sized tomatoes
- 1 can of 20-ounce green jackfruit drained and rinsed up
- ½ to ¾ teaspoon of flavored vinegar according to your taste
- 1 and a ½ cups of water

<u>How To</u>

1. Set your pot to Sauté mode and add oil, allow the oil to heat up
2. Add cumin, nigella seeds and mustard, cook for 1 minute
3. Once they start to pop, add onion, ginger and garlic with a pinch of flavored vinegar
4. Add coriander, black pepper, turmeric and give it a nice mix
5. Add pureed tomato and cook for 2 minutes
6. Add jackfruit, water and flavored vinegar

7. Lock up the lid and cook on HIGH pressure for 7-8 minutes
8. Release the pressure naturally
9. Shred your cooked jackfruit using a spatula and serve
10. Enjoy!

<u>Nutrition (Per Serving)</u>

- Calories: 312
- Fat: 5g
- Carbohydrates: 61g
- Protein: 8g

Chapter 12: Soup and Stews Recipes

Mesmerizing Corn Chowder

Serving: 2

Prep Time: 15 minutes

Cook Time: 15 minutes

Ingredients

- 5 whole potatoes, peeled and chopped
- 3 cups frozen corn
- 3 garlic cloves, minced
- 1 red pepper, chopped
- 1 yellow onion, chopped
- 2 teaspoon paprika
- 2 cups vegetable broth
- 1 can light coconut milk
- Vinegar as needed
- Green onion, red pepper and cilantro for garnish

How To

1. Chop up the onion and mince garlic, add them to your Instant Pot
2. Chop up the potatoes and pepper and keep them on the side for later use
3. Set your pot to Sauté mode and add ¼ cup of broth
4. Take a spatula and keep stirring the onion and garlic, Sauté for 5 minutes
5. Add the rest of the ingredients and potatoes
6. Lock up the lid and cook on HIGH pressure for 8 minutes
7. Release the pressure naturally over 10 minutes
8. Take an immersion blender and puree
9. Serve over rice and garnish with a bit of green onion, pepper and corn

Nutrition (Per Serving)

- Calories: 50
- Fat: 4.4g
- Carbohydrates: 3.1g
- Protein: 0.7g

Easy Beef Stew

Serving: 2

Prep Time: 10 minutes

Cook Time: 25 minutes

Ingredients

- 1-pound beef meat, cubed
- 1 tablespoon of olive oil
- 1 tablespoon flour
- Pinch of pepper and salt
- 1 small yellow onion, chopped
- 1 garlic clove, minced
- 3 tablespoon red wine
- 1 celery stalk, chopped
- 2 small carrots, chopped
- ½ tablespoon of tomato paste
- 1 cup beef stock
- 2 tablespoon parsley, chopped

How To

1. Take a bowl and add meat, salt, pepper, flour and toss
2. Set your pot to Sauté mode and add oil, allow the oil to heat up
3. Add beef, brown all sides
4. Transfer the cooked meat to a bowl and keep it on the side
5. Add wine to your Instant Pot
6. Cook on Sauté mode for a few minutes
7. Return beef to your pot, add carrots, onion, garlic, potatoes, celery, stock, tomato paste and stir
8. Close the lid and cook on HIGH pressure for 20 minutes
9. Release pressure naturally over 10 minutes

10. Open lid and add parsley
11. Stir stew and divide between 2 bowls
12. Enjoy!

Nutrition (Per Serving)

- Calories: 312
- Fat: 2g
- Carbohydrates: 4g
- Protein: 6g

Carrot and Potato Ultimate Soup

Serving: 2

Prep Time: 15 minutes

Cook Time: 10 minutes

Ingredients

- 5 medium potatoes, peeled and chopped
- 8 carrots, peeled and chopped
- ½ of yellow onion, chopped
- 3 garlic cloves, minced
- 2 cups fresh kale, minced
- 1 tablespoon of curry powder
- 1 teaspoon of cayenne pepper
- 4 cups of water
- 2 cups of vegetable broth

How To

1. Mince up garlic and chop up the onions
2. Add ¼ cup of water to the pot and set the pot to Sauté mode
3. Add onions and garlic and Sauté for 5 minutes
4. Add vegetable broth, cayenne, powdered peanut butter and curry powder
5. Stir everything well
6. Add water and Sauté for 2 minutes
7. Add the remaining ingredients (except kale) and seal the lid
8. Cook on HIGH pressure for 8 minutes
9. Release the pressure naturally
10. Open the lid and take an immersion blender to puree the soup
11. Add chopped up kale and mix well
12. Serve and enjoy!

Nutrition (Per Serving)

- Calories: 128
- Fat: 4g
- Carbohydrates: 20g
- Protein: 15

Pumpkin and Walnut Chilis

Serving: 2

Prep Time: 10 minutes

Cook Time: 30 minutes

Ingredients

For Chili

- 1 can of 28-ounce fire roasted tomatoes
- ½ onion, minced
- 3 garlic cloves, minced
- 2 poblano pepper, chopped
- 2-3 chipotle pepper, chopped
- 2 cups walnuts, chopped
- 1 cup of red lentils
- 1 cup of bulgur
- 2 tablespoon of chili powder
- 1 tablespoon of smoked paprika
- 1 tablespoon of flavored vinegar
- 6 cups of broth/ water

Extra addition

- 1 can of 14 ounces of pumpkin puree
- 2-3 cans of 14-ounce black beans, rinse and drained

How To

1. Add the ingredients listed under chili to your Instant Pot
2. Lock up the lid and cook on SOUP mode for 30 minutes
3. Release the pressure naturally over 10 minutes
4. Stir in black beans and pumpkin puree

5. Season with a bit of flavored vinegar and spices
6. Stir and serve over avocado rice
7. Enjoy!

Nutrition (Per Serving)

- Calories: 307
- Fat: 12g
- Carbohydrates: 40g
- Protein: 12

Pork Cheek Stew

Serving: 2

Prep Time: 10 minutes

Cook Time: 45 minutes

Ingredients

- 4 pound of pork cheeks
- 2 tablespoons of avocado oil
- 1 and a ½ cups of chicken broth
- 8 ounce of cremini mushroom
- 1 large sized leek cut up into ½ inch chunks
- 1 small onion, diced
- 6 garlic cloves, peeled
- 1 teaspoon of sea salt
- Juice of ½ lemon

How To

1. Set your pot to Sauté mode and add oil
2. Cut up the cheeks into 2 x 3 inch even pieces and add them to the Pot
3. Sear them until nicely browned
4. Pour broth over the browned cheeks alongside mushroom, onion, leek, garlic, sea salt
5. Lock up the lid and cook on HIGH pressure for 45 minutes using the MEAT and STEWS mode
6. Release the pressure naturally and shred the meat
7. Stir the meat well with the sauce and serve!

Nutrition (Per Serving)

- Calories: 260
- Fat: 14g
- Carbohydrates: 14g

Ravaging Buffalo Chicken Soup

Serving: 2

Prep Time: 10 minutes

Cook Time: 10 minutes

Ingredients

- 2 chicken breast, boneless and skinless
- 3 cups chicken bone broth
- ½ cup celery, diced
- ¼ cup onion, diced
- 1 garlic clove, chopped
- 1 tablespoon of ranch dressing
- 2 tablespoons butter
- 1/3 cup hot sauce
- 2 cups cheddar, shredded
- 1 cup heavy cream

How To

1. Add all of the ingredients to your Instant Pot except cream and cheese
2. Lock up the lid and cook on HIGH pressure for 10 minutes
3. Perform a quick release
4. Remove the chicken and shred them, return to your soup
5. Add heavy cream, cheese and stir well

Nutrition (Per Serving)

- Calories: 378
- Fat: 19g
- Carbohydrates: 19g
- Protein: 27g

Chapter 13: Desserts Recipes

Creative Pinna Colada

Serving: 2

Prep Time: 5 minutes

Cook Time: 15 minutes

Ingredients

- 1 cup Arborio Rice
- 1 and a ½ cup water
- 1 cup maple syrup
- 1 can coocnut milk
- 2/3 cup pineapple, crushed
- 1 tablespoon of cinnamon

How To

1. Add water and rice to your Instant Pot
2. Lock up the lid and cook on LOW pressure for 12 minutes
3. Perform a quick release
4. Add maple syrup, half of the coconut milk, cinnamon and pineapple
5. Give it a stir and allow it to cool
6. Add remaining milk and enjoy!

Nutrition (Per Serving)

- Calories: 414
- Fat: 5g
- Carbohydrates: 21g
- Protein: 15g

Braised Apple Platter

Serving: 2

Prep Time: 15 minutes

Cook Time: 10 minutes

Ingredients

- 2 apples, cored
- ½ cup water
- ½ cup red wine
- 3 tablespoon demerara sugar
- 2 tablespoons of raisins
- ½ a teaspoon ground cinnamon

How To

1. Add water to your Instant Pot
2. Add apples
3. Pour wine on top and sprinkle sugar, cinnamon and raisins
4. Lock lid and cook on HIGH pressure for 10 minutes
5. Perform quick release
6. Transfer apples onto serving plate and top with cooking liquid
7. Enjoy!

Nutrition (Per Serving)

- Calories: 245
- Fat: 0.5g
- Carbohydrates: 53g
- Protein: 1g

A Glass Full of Soy Milk

Serving: 2

Prep Time: 10 minutes

Cook Time: 25 minutes

<u>Ingredients</u>

- ½ cup of organic yellow soy bean
- 5 cups of water
- ½ teaspoon of stevia
- 1 piece of vanilla bean extract
- 1 pinch of cinnamon

<u>How To</u>

1. You need to soak the beans under water for about 36 hours prior to making the recipe
2. Strain the beans and replace old water with new after every 12 hours
3. Take a cutting board and chop up the soy beans
4. Take a small sized bowl and add the chopped-up beans alongside ½ a cup of water
5. Add the mix to your blender and puree for 90 seconds
6. Pour the puree into your pot and add 5 cups of water
7. Give it a nice stir
8. Set your pot to Sauté mode and allow it to reach boiling point (foam will appear)
9. Stir it well and lock up the lid. Cook for 9 minutes under HIGH pressure
10. Allow the pressure to release naturally
11. Take another bowl and add stevia, vanilla bean extract, cinnamon and mix well
12. Open the lid and carefully strain the liquid into this bowl
13. Give it a nice stir and your milk is ready!
14. Enjoy

<u>Nutrition (Per Serving)</u>

- Calories: 131

- Fats: 4.3g
- Carbs:15g
- Protein:23g

Sweetest Mango Rice for Two

Serving: 2

Prep Time: 5 minutes

Cook Time: 20 minutes

Ingredients

- 1 cup of white jasmine rice
- 1 and a ¼ cup and an extra 1/3 cup of light sweetened coconut milk
- 1 cup of frozen mango chunks
- 2 tablespoons of brown sugar
- Black sesame seeds

How To

1. Measure out 1 cup of jasmine rice and 1 and a ¼ cup of light coconut milk and add them to the pot
2. Add mango chunks on top and a bit of coconut milk as well
3. Lock up the lid and cook on HIGH pressure for 4 minutes
4. Release the pressure naturally over 10 minutes
5. Add extra coconut milk and mix
6. Spoon up the rice and mango mix to serving bowls
7. Sprinkle a bit of brown sugar and some sesame seeds, enjoy!

Nutrition (Per Serving)

- Calories: 50
- Fat: 4.4g
- Carbohydrates: 3.1g
- Protein: 0.7g

Juicy Strawberry Cobbler

Serving: 2

Prep Time: 15 minutes

Cook Time: 12 minutes

Ingredients

- 1 and a ¼ cups all purpose flour
- ½ cup granulated sugar
- 1 and ½ teaspoons baking powder
- ¾ cup milk
- 1/3 cup butter, softened
- 1 teaspoon vanilla extract
- ¾ cup fresh strawberries, hulled and sliced

How To

1. Take a large bowl and add the listed ingredients (except strawberries)
2. Whisk well
3. Gently fold in strawberry slices
4. Transfer mix to greased pan
5. Arrange the trivet in bottom of your Pot
6. Add a cup of water
7. Arrange pan on top of trivet
8. Lock up the lid and cook on HIGH pressure for 12 minutes
9. Naturally release pressure for 5 minutes then perform quick release
10. Remove pan and let it cool

Nutrition (Per Serving)

- Calories: 816
- Fat: 33g
- Carbohydrates: 120g

Conclusion

I can't express how honored I am to think that you found my book interesting and informative enough to read it all through to the end.

From here on out, I would encourage you to keep experimenting with different ingredients and walk towards the path of becoming the next master of the Instant Pot!

I thank you again for purchasing this book and I hope that you had as much fun reading it as I had writing it.

Made in the USA
Middletown, DE
08 June 2018